'So are you
to my thoughts
as food to life'

William Shakespeare 1564–1616, *Sonnet 75*

TUDOR COOKERY

Recipes & History

by
Peter Brears

with a Foreword by
Loyd Grossman OBE

ENGLISH HERITAGE

Front cover: Detail from *William Brooke, 10th Lord Cobham and his Family,* 1567 (panel) by Master of the Countess of Warwick, Longleat House, Wiltshire

Endpapers: Illustrations from the *Ordinance of the Bakers of York:* measuring flour; boulting the flour; kneading in a dough trough; making and weighing small loaves; pricking the loaves; baking the bread in a bee-hive oven

Published by English Heritage, Kemble Drive, Swindon SN2 2GZ

Copyright © English Heritage and Peter Brears
First published 1985
Revised edition 2003

ISBN 1 85074 868 3

C60, 1/04, Product code 50815

Edited by Susan Kelleher
Designed by Pauline Hull
Picture research by Elaine Willis
Brought to press by Andrew McLaren
Printed in England by Bath Press

CONTENTS

FOREWORD

Would the pyramids have been built without the recently invented bread to efficiently feed the workforce? Food is a common denominator between us all, and a potent link with our ancestors, just as much as an ancient parish church or a listed house.

I am delighted to contribute a Foreword to English Heritage's series of historic cookery books, which neatly combine two of my passions – history and food. Most of us no longer have to catch or grow our own food before eating it, but the continuing daily need for sustenance still powerfully links us with our earliest forebears. We may not like the thought of Roman fish sauce made from fermented entrails (until we next add oyster sauce to a Chinese beef dish), but we can only sigh with recognition at a Jacobean wife's exhortation to 'let yor butter bee scalding hott in yor pan' before pouring in the beaten eggs for an omelette. The Roman penchant for dormice cooked in milk doesn't resonate with us now, but a dish of pears in red wine features at modern dinner parties just as it did in medieval times.

Food and cooking have inevitably changed down the centuries, as modern cookers have supplanted open hearths, and increased wealth and speedy transport have opened up modern tastes and palates to the widest range of ingredients and cuisines. But it's worth remembering that it was the Romans who gave us onions, sugar was an expensive luxury in the 16th century as was tea in the 17th, the tomato only became popular in Europe in the 19th century and even in the 1950s avocados and red peppers were still exotic foreign imports.

I urge you to experiment with the recipes in these books which cover over 2,000 years, and hope you enjoy, as I have, all that is sometimes strange and often familiar about the taste of times past.

Loyd Grossman OBE
Former Commissioner of English Heritage
Chairman of the Campaign for Museums

INTRODUCTION

The 16th century, the colourful flowering of Tudor England, has bequeathed to posterity a whole series of rich and potent images, full of spectacle and a robust *joie de vivre*. In it we see a largely feudal state boisterously adopting the fashions of Renaissance Europe in all aspects of its courtly life and culture. The paintings of Nicholas Hilliard and his contemporaries show the lavish and colourful dress of men and women who enjoyed the music of Morley, Dowland and Campion, the poetry of Spenser and Sidney, or the plays of Marlowe and Shakespeare. The houses they occupied, from the soaring honey-coloured splendours of Burghley, Hardwick and Longleat to a host of brick and half-timbered country manor houses, similarly evoke the essential spirit of this period. Most potent of all, however, are the portraits of Henry VIII and Elizabeth I, a Renaissance prince and a sacred virgin presiding over a new age of development and increasing trade. The magnificence of their costumes, the fabulous richness of their apartments, and the elaborate ceremonies of their courts were all essential elements in leading and controlling a country still divided into religious factions and under constant threat of insurrection or invasion.

Against this background, cookery may appear to be of trifling importance, but it too reflects the influence of Renaissance Europe, in addition to providing evidence of the sumptuous entertainments held largely for political reasons both at court and in the larger houses. A great variety of documentary sources ranging from estate papers to plays and poems, refer to the preparation of food, but probably our greatest debt of gratitude is to Edward White and his fellow London publishers of the late 16th century. By collecting together and publishing a series of cookery books they have preserved a unique body of information which is still available to us today.

In general terms, the foodstuffs enjoyed in 16th-century England were almost identical to those of the medieval period. Roast and boiled meat, poultry, fish, pottages, frumenty, bread, ale, wine and to a much lesser extent, fruit and vegetables, formed the basis of the diet of the upper classes. The range and qualities of these comestibles are best described in Andrew Boorde's

Opposite: Elizabeth I by Biagio Rebecca (1735–1808), Audley End House, Essex

Compendyous Regyment or Dyetary of Health of 1542, where he writes of venison:

> *A lordes dysshe, good for an Englisshe man, for it doth anymate hym to be as he is, whiche is, stronge and hardy …; Beef is a good meate for an Englysshe man, so be it the beest be yonge, & that it be not kowe-fleshe; yf it be moderatly powdered [i.e. salted] that the groose blode by salt may be exhaustyd, it doth make an Englysshe man stronge; Veal is good and easily digested; Brawn [boar's meat] is an usual meate in winter amonges Englisshe men; Bacon is good for carters and plowmen, the whiche be ever labouringe in the earth or dung … I do say that coloppes [slices of bacon] and egges is as holsome for them as a talowe candell is good for a blereyed mare … Potage is not so moch used in al Crystendom as it is used in Englande. Potage is made of the lyquor in the which fleshe is soden [boiled] in, with puttyng-to chopped herbes and otemel and salt. Fyrmente is made of whete and mylke, in the which yf flesshe be soden … it doth nourysshe, and it doth strength a man. Of all nacyons and*

countres, England is beste servyed of Fysshe, not onely of al maner of see-fysshe, but also of fresshe-water fysshe, and al maner of sortes of salte-fysshe.

He also advised his readers to eat vegetables such as turnips, parsnips, carrots, onions, leeks, garlic and radishes, and fruit in the form of mellow red apples. Even so, raw vegetables and fruit were still regarded with great suspicion by most Tudor diners who felt they were likely to be the cause of sickness and disease. It was for this reason that the sale of fruit was banned in the streets during the plague of 1569.

In addition to the apples, pears, plums, cherries and woodland strawberries which had been grown here for centuries, new fruit from southern Europe were now introduced into the gardens of the wealthy.

'Beware of green sallettes & rawe fruytes for they wyll make your soverayne seke.'

Boke of Kervynge, 1500

Henry VIII wanted to enjoy a wider variety of fruit than that which was available in England in the early 16th century. He therefore instructed his fruiterer, Richard Harris, to travel to France and the Low Countries to bring back grafts of different apples, pears and cherries. Harris laid down the first large commercial orchard at Teynham in Kent, *'the chiefe mother of all the orchards for all those kinds of fruites'*. Before long 'the garden of England' was characterised by its extensive orchards.

Opposite and right: The Golden Reinette apple which was introduced to England in 1533 by Richard Harris and still flourishes in the orchards of the Brogdale Horticultural Trust in Kent

13

A fruit called 'xitomati' meaning 'plump' had been cultivated by the Incas and Aztecs since as early as 700AD but it was not until the 16th century, after the conquest of much of the New World by the Spanish conquistadors, that tomato seeds reached Europe. Here, there was a mixed reception for this new addition to the diet. Some nations, such as the French and Italians, believed it to have aphrodisiac qualities and named it the 'love apple' or the 'golden apple', while the Germans called it the 'apple of Paradise'. However, the British were far less enthusiastic and many believed it to be poisonous because of its red colour.

These included quinces, apricots, raspberries, red and black currants, melons, and even pomegranates, oranges and lemons. The last were never really successful however, and citrus fruits continued to be imported in large quantities to serve the luxury market.

As a result of the mid-16th century Spanish exploitation of their great South American colonies, a number of rare and exotic vegetables slowly began to arrive in Elizabethan England. Tomatoes came from Mexico and kidney beans from Peru, for example, while the potato originated from Chile and the Andes. Centuries were to pass before the true value of these new foods was fully appreciated, however, and they continued to be served largely as unusual delicacies in the well-to-do households.

Boiling meat in a cauldron

A much more popular introduction from the New World was the turkey, a native of Mexico and of Central America, which had already found its way on to English tables by the 1540s. One of Sebastian Cabot's commanders, Sir William Strickland of the East Riding village of Boynton, claimed to have brought the first turkeys into this country, and therefore adopted a white turkey-cock with a black beak and red wattle as his family crest. Birds of this type were available in the London markets of the mid-16th century, and from that time onwards regularly appeared at important feasts and entertainments.

Of all the changes concerning food in the 16th century, the most important and influential was the growing popularity of sugar. Now, in addition to the old-established sources of supply in Morocco and Barbary, increasing quantities were coming into Europe from the new Portuguese and Spanish plantations in the West Indies, some arriving here through the activities of our privateers. From the 1540s a refinery in London was carrying out the final stages of purification, converting the coarse sugar into white crystalline cones weighing up to 7 kilos (14lbs). These could then be used to prepare a great variety of sweetmeats, crystallised fruits, preserves and syrups, in addition to being employed in seasoning meat, fish, and vegetable dishes.

The national annual consumption of sugar averaged no more than 450g (1lb) a head during this period, but the great majority of this was eaten by the aristocracy, who rapidly began to suffer from tooth decay. As Paul Hentzer noted, even Queen Elizabeth's teeth were black, 'a defect the English seem subject to,

A woodcut of a confectioner pounding sugar for sweetmeats to supply the growing demand

from their too great use of sugar'. The ashes of rosemary leaves or powdered alabaster rubbed over the teeth with the finger helped to prevent tooth decay, as did the use of elaborate toothpicks of precious metals, often worn in the hat. Expert barbers might also use metal instruments to scrape the teeth, then apply aqua fortis (nitric acid) to bleach them to whiteness. As Sir Hugh Platt warned, this treatment could be disastrous, for after a few applications a lady may 'be forced to borrow a ranke of teeth to eate her dinner, unless her gums doe help her the better'.

> 'A great man,
> I'll warrant;
> I know by
> the picking
> on's teeth.'
>
> William Shakespeare
> 1564–1616,
> Clown in *The Winter's Tale*

Opposite: Raspberries from southern Europe were introduced into the diet in Tudor times

Recipes

STEWED MUTTON

*To boyle a Leg of Mutton with
Lemmons: When your mutton is half
boyled, take it up, cut it in small
peeces, put it into a Pipkin and cover
it close, and put therto the best of the
broth, a much as shall cover your
Mutton, your Lemmons being sliced
very thin and quartered and
corance; put in pepper groce beaten,
and so let them boile together, and
when they be well boiled, seson it
with a little vergious, Sugar, Pepper
groce beaten, and a little sanders, so
lay it in fine dishes upon sops, it will
make IV messe for the table.*

450 g (1 lb) lean lamb or mutton
1 lemon
425 ml (³/4 pt) stock

50 g (2 oz) currants
1.5 ml (¹/4 tsp) pepper
5 ml (1 tsp) wine vinegar
15 ml (1 tbls) sugar
red food colouring

Cut the mutton into cubes. Slice the
lemons thinly, then cut each slice into
four quarters. Pour the stock into a
saucepan, then add the mutton, lemon,
currants and pepper, and simmer for
1¹/2 hours, until the meat is tender. The
vinegar, sugar and red food colouring
may be stirred in just before serving.
The resulting dish has a pleasant sharp
lemon flavour, and is extremely
palatable.

*A.W. : A Book of Cookrye Very
necessary for all such as delight therin*

THICK MUTTON STEW

For to make charmerchande: Take coostes of motton chopped and putte theym in a fayre potte and sette it upon the fyre with clene water and boyle it welle; and thanne take percely and sage and bete it in a morter with brede and drawe it uppe withe the brothe and put it in the potte with the fresshe flesshe and lette it boyle welle togyder; and salte it and serve it.

450 g (1 lb) lean mutton
575 ml (1 pt) water
100 g (4 oz) fresh brown
   breadcrumbs
5 ml (1 tsp) salt
5 ml (1 tsp) dried parsley
5 ml (1 tsp) dried sage

Cut the mutton into small cubes. Place in a saucepan with the water and simmer gently for 1½-2 hours until tender, then add the rest of the ingredients and stir until the bread has fully absorbed all the juices to form a thick delicately flavoured stew.

The Boke of Cokery

MUTTON IN BEER

To Stewe Stekes of Mutton: Take a legge of mutton and cot it in small slices, and put it in a chafer, and put therto a pottell of ale, and scome it cleane then putte therto seven or eyghte onions thyn slyced, and after they have boyled one hour, putte therto a dyshe of swete butter, and so lette them boyle tyll they be tender, and then put therto a lyttel peper and salte.

Bone the meat, trim off the skin and excess fat, and cut into thin slices across the grain. Place in a heavy pan with the beer and onions, cover and simmer for an hour before adding the salt, pepper and butter. Simmer for a further 20-30 minutes until tender. Serve on cubes of crustless bread in a deep dish.

A Proper Newe Book of Cokerye

900 g (2 lb) leg of lamb or mutton
575 ml (I pint) brown ale
I large or 2 small onions, thinly
**   sliced**
5 ml (I tsp) salt
pepper to taste
25 g (I oz) butter
bread slices, cut into crustless
**   cubes, to serve**

Stewed steaks later developed into 'Scotch collops', one of the most popular dishes of the 17th and 18th centuries.

REAL MINCE PIE

For Pyes of Mutton or Beefe: Shred your meat and Suet togither fine, season it with cloves, mace, Pepper, and some Saffron, great Raisins, Corance and prunes, and so put it into your Pyes.

**700 g (1½ lb) lean mutton
   or beef**
100 g (4 oz) suet
2.5 ml (½ tsp) ground cloves
5 ml (1 tsp) ground mace
2.5 ml (½ tsp) black pepper
a pinch of saffron
50 g (2 oz) raisins
50 g (2 oz) currants
50 g (2 oz) stoned prunes, chopped

For the pastry:
450 g (1 lb) plain flour
10 ml (2 tsps) salt

100 g (4 oz) lard
150 ml (¼ pt) water
60 ml (4 tbls) milk

For the glaze:
**15 ml (1 tbls) each of butter,
   sugar and rosewater melted
   together**

Mince the meat, and mix in the suet, spices, pepper, saffron and dried fruit. To make the pastry, sift the flour and salt together into a large mixing bowl and make a well in the centre. Heat the lard, water and milk until boiling and pour into the well. Quickly beat the mixture together with a spoon to form a soft dough, and knead until smooth on a lightly floured board. Cut off a quarter of the pastry, and keep covered until required to make the lid.

Mould the larger piece of pastry to form the base and sides of the pie within a 20 cm (8 in) diameter, 5 cm (2 in) deep loose-bottomed tin. Pack the meat into the pie and dampen the edges of the pie wall. Roll out the remaining pastry to make a lid and firmly press into place. Trim the edges, using the surplus pastry for decoration, and cut a hole in the centre of the lid. Bake in the centre of the oven at gas mark 7, 220°C (425°F) for 15 minutes, then reduce the temperature to gas mark 4, 180°C (350°F) for a further 1 1/4 hours. Remove the sides of the tin, brush with the glaze, and return to the oven for a further 15 minutes. Serve cold.

This pie, with its combination of meat, suet and dried fruit, is the predecessor of today's 'mince pies', in which the meat has been totally replaced by the fruit. It still makes an excellent dish for Christmastime, providing a substantial and finely flavoured dish for a buffet supper.

A.W. : *A Book of Cookrye Very necessary for all such as delight therin*

BEEF PASTRY, BAKED LIKE VENISON

To make red deere: Take a legge of beef, and cut out all the sinewes clean, then take a roling pin and all to beate it, then perboile it, and when you have so doon lard it very thick, then lay it in wine or Vinegar for two or three howers, or a whole night, then take it out & season it with peper, salt, cloves and maice, then put it into your past, & so bake it.

700 g (1½ lb) good-quality steak
350 ml (½ bottle) claret
strips of bacon fat or pork
shortcrust pastry made with 350 g
  (12 oz) plain flour and 175 g
  (6 oz) butter
10 ml (2 tsps) salt
5 ml (1 tsp) pepper
2.5 ml (½ tsp) ground cloves
5 ml (1 tsp) ground mace

a little gravy or 15 ml (1 tbls) each
  butter, rosewater and sugar

Trim the fat from the steak, beat it, and soak in the claret for 24 hours. Drain, and use a larding needle to insert small strips of raw bacon or pork fat into one side of the steak. Roll out the pastry into a large rectangle. Arrange the steak on one half, season it with the salt, pepper and spices, fold the remaining pastry over the top, dampen and seal the edges, and place on a greased baking sheet. Bake at gas mark 6, 200°C (400°F) for 15 minutes, then reduce the temperature to gas mark 4, 180°C (350°F) for a further 50-60 minutes. Before removing pastry, it may be glazed with either a little gravy or a mixture of butter, rosewater and sugar melted together. Serve either hot or cold.

Thomas Dawson: *The good huswifes Jewell, pt. 1*

SAVOURY TONGUE PIE

To bake a Neatstung: Seeth your Neats tung very tender and slice it in diamond slices, wash it with vergious, season it with Pepper and salt, sinamon and ginger, then lay it into your coffin with Corance, whole Mace, Onions being very small minced, with Marrow or else very sweet butter, some Sugar & some dates being very small minced, and put therein some vergious.

1 small ox tongue, weighing
   1–1.4 kg (2½–3 lb)
10 ml (2 tsps) salt
5 ml (1 tsp) pepper
5 ml (1 tsp) cinnamon
5 ml (1 tsp) ground ginger
5 ml (1 tsp) blade mace
1 small onion, minced
100 g (4 oz) currants

50 g (2 oz) dates, stoned and
   minced
50 g (2 oz) butter
50 g (2 oz) sugar
30 ml (2 tbls) wine vinegar

For the pastry:
450 g (1 lb) plain flour
10 ml (2 tsps) salt
100 g (4 oz) lard
150 ml (¼ pt) water
60 ml (4 tbls) milk

For the glaze:
5 ml (1 tsp) each of butter, sugar
   and rosewater, melted together

Place the tongue in a pan, cover with water and bring to the boil, carefully skimming off the frothy scum which rises to the surface. Continue to simmer for a further 2 hours, then drain the tongue, plunge it into cold water, and peel off the skin. Slice the tongue. Then cut the slices into long diamond-shaped pieces, and thoroughly mix in a bowl with the remaining pie ingredients. To make the pastry, sift the flour and salt together into a large mixing bowl and make a well in the centre. Heat the lard, water and milk until boiling and pour into the well. Quickly beat the mixture together with a spoon to form a soft dough, and knead until smooth on a lightly floured board. Cut off a quarter of the pastry and keep covered until required to make the lid. Mould the larger piece of pastry to form the base and sides of the pie within a 18 or 20 cm (7 or 8 in) cake tin, preferably with a loose bottom, and pack the filling inside. Dampen the edges of the pie wall. Roll out the remaining pastry to make a lid and firmly press into place. Rim the edges, using the surplus for decoration, and cut a hole in the centre of lid. Bake in the centre of the oven at gas mark 7, 220°C (425°F) for 15 minutes, then reduce the temperature to gas mark 4, 180°C (350°F) for a further 1³/₄ hours. Carefully remove the sides of the tin, brush with the glaze, and return to the oven for a further 15 minutes. Serve cold.

A.W. : *A Book of Cookrye Very necessary for all such as delight therin*

SMOTHERED RABBIT

How to smeare a Rabbet or a necke of Mutton: Take a Pipkin, a porrenger of water, two or three spoonefuls of Vergis, ten Onions pilled, and if they be great quarter them, mingle as much Pepper and salte as will season them, and rub it upon the meat, if it be a rabbit: put in a peece of butter in the bellye and a peece in the broth, and a few Currans if you wil, stop your pot close and seeth it with a softe fier but no fier under the bottome, then when it is sodden serve it in upon soppes & lay a few Barberies upon the dishe.

900 g (2 lb) onions
50 g (2 oz) currants
1 rabbit, jointed
salt and pepper
275 ml ('/2 pt) water
45 ml (3 tbls) wine vinegar
50 g (2 oz) butter
bread slices, cut into large crustless cubes, to serve
barberries or redcurrants, to garnish

Peel and quarter the onions. Arrange with the currants over the base of a large saucepan or casserole. Rub the rabbit joints with salt and pepper, and embed them in the onions and currants. Add the remaining ingredients, and simmer on a low heat for 1-1 1/2 hours until the rabbit is cooked. Prepare a deep dish by lining it with sops – large crustless cubes of bread – and pour in the smothered rabbit. Garnish the dish with the barberries or redcurrants.

The Good Hous-wives Treasurie

29

SWEET CHICKEN PÂTÉ

To make a mortis: Take almonds and blanche them, and beat them in a morter, and boyle a Chicken, and take al the flesh of him, and beate it, and straine them together, with milke and water, and so put them into a pot, and put in Suger, and stirre them still, and when it hath boyled a good while, take it of, and set it a cooling in a payle of water, and straine it againe with Rose water into a dish.

½ chicken
50 g (2 oz) blanched almonds
150 ml (¼ pt) milk
15 ml (1 tbls) sugar
15 ml (1 tbls) rosewater

Put the chicken in a saucepan, cover with water and boil until tender – about 45 minutes. Drain, and pick all the meat from the bones. While the chicken is boiling, use either a mortar and pestle or a blender to grind the almonds and milk together to form a smooth paste. Grind the cooked chicken into this paste, then place the mixture in a saucepan with the sugar and cook over a gentle heat for 10-15 minutes, stirring continuously. Cool the saucepan in a bowl of cold water, beat in the rosewater, and finally fork the resulting pâté either down into a deep bowl, or into a symmetrical shape on a plate ready for the table.

Thomas Dawson: *The good huswifes Jewell, pt. 1*

This 'mortrews', a survival of the medieval standing pottages, makes a pleasant and interesting addition to any buffet or summer salad.

CAPON WITH ORANGE OR LEMON SAUCE

To boile a Capon with Orenges and Lemmons: Take Orenges or Lemmons pilled, and cutte them the long way, and if you can keep your cloves whole and put them into your best broth of Mutton or Capon with prunes or currants and three or fowre dates, and when these have been well sodden put whole pepper, great mace, a good piece of suger, some rose water, and either white or claret Wine, and let al these seeth together a while, & so serve it upon soppes with your capon.

1 capon or chicken
575 ml (1 pint) chicken stock
50 g (2 oz) currants
4 dates
about 225 g (8 oz) oranges, mandarins or lemons
2.5 ml (½ tsp) black peppercorns

5 ml (1 tsp) blade mace
45 ml (3 tbls) sugar
15 ml (1 tbls) rosewater
150 ml (¼ pint) white wine or claret
225 g (8 oz) white bread, cut into large crustless cubes

Put the capon or chicken in a pan, cover with water and boil until tender. Drain 575 ml (1 pint) stock from bird, and simmer for 5 minutes with the currants, dates and fruit, peeled and divided into individual segments. Then add the remaining ingredients (white wine being preferable when using lemons), simmer for a further 5-10 minutes, and pour over the bird arranged on a bed of bread cubes in a large dish.

Thomas Dawson:
The good huswifes Jewell, pt. 1

FRIED WHITING

To fry Whitings: First flay them and wash them clean and seale them, that doon, lap them in floure and fry them in Butter and oyle. Then to serve them, mince apples and onions and fry them, then put them into a vessel with white wine, vergious, salt, pepper, clove & mace, and boile them together on the Coles, and serve it upon the Whitings.

225 g (8 oz) apples or onions, minced
butter or oil for frying
275 ml ($^1/_2$ pt) white wine
15 ml (1 tbls) wine vinegar
5 ml (1 tsp) salt
1.5 ml ($^1/_4$ tsp) pepper
1.5 ml ($^1/_4$ tsp) ground mace
a pinch of ground cloves
450–700 g (1–1$^1/_2$ lb) whiting fillets

> 'A plague o'these pickle herring!'
>
> William Shakespeare 1564-1616, *Twelfth Night*, 1601

Fry the apples or onions in a little butter or oil in a small saucepan until thoroughly cooked, but not browned. Stir in the wine, vinegar, salt, pepper and spices. Allow to cook for a few minutes, then keep hot ready for use. Remove any skin from the fillets, dust them with flour, fry in butter or oil for 5-10 minutes, and serve with the sauce.

A.W. : *A Book of Cookrye Very necessary for all such as delight therin*

TROUT PASTIES

A Troute baked or minced: Take a Troute and seeth him, then take out all the bones, then mince it fine with three or four dates minced with it, seasoning it with Ginger, and Sinamon, and a quantitie of Suger and Butter, put all these together, working them fast, then take your fine paste, and cut in three corner waies in a small bignesse, of four or five coffins in a dish, then lay your stuffe in them, close them, and so bake them and in the serving of them baste the covers with a little butter, and then cast a little blaunch pouder on them, and so serve it foorth.

1 trout
3 or 4 dates, chopped
1.5 ml (¹/4 tsp) ground ginger
1.5 ml (¹/4 tsp) cinnamon
7.5 ml (¹/2 tbls) sugar
50 g (2 oz) butter

For the pastry:
75 g (3 oz) butter
100 g (4 oz) plain flour
1 egg, beaten

Place the trout in a saucepan, cover with boiling water, and simmer for 10-15 minutes until tender. Drain the trout, remove the flesh from the bones, and blend it with the remaining ingredients to form a soft paste. To make the pastry, rub the butter into the flour, then stir continuously while adding the beaten egg to form a soft dough which can be lightly kneaded with the hands. Turn out on to a floured board, roll out, and cut into four or five large triangles. Place a portion of the trout paste in the centre of each triangle, bringing the corners up over the paste to form triangular envelopes. Moisten the edges, carefully seal them together, place on a baking sheet and bake at gas mark 7, 220°C (425°F) for 15 minutes, then reduce the heat to gas mark 4, 180°C (350°F) and bake for a further 10 minutes. The pasties may then be brushed with melted butter and dusted with caster sugar and cinnamon, although this might be found too sweet for present-day tastes.

Thomas Dawson:
The good huswifes Jewell, pt. 2

'Suppose a man were eating rotten stockfish, the every smell of which would choke another, and yet believed it a dish for the gods, what difference is there as to his happiness?'

Erasmus 1466-1536

CHEESE TART

To make a Tarte of Cheese: Take good fine paste and drive it as thin as you can. Then take cheese, pare it, mince it, and bray it in a morter with the yolks of Egs til it be like paste, then put it in a faire dish with clarified butter and then put it abroad into your paste and cover it with a faire cut cover, and so bake it; that doon, serve it forth.

225 g (8 oz) Cheshire or similar cheese
50 g (2 oz) butter
3 egg yolks

For the pastry:
75 g (3 oz) butter
100 g (4 oz) plain flour
1 egg, beaten

To make the pastry, rub the butter into the flour, and slowly add the egg, stirring continuously until the dough can be lightly kneaded with the hands. Roll out rather more than half the pastry and use it to line a shallow ovenproof 25 cm (10 in) plate. Grate the cheese finely, and blend it with the butter and the egg yolks to form a smooth, moist paste. Fill the pastry-lined plate with this mixture and moisten the pastry edges. Roll out the remaining pastry to cover, and seal tightly. Press down the edges with the tines of a fork, then trim. Pierce the lid and bake at gas mark 7, 220°C (425°F) for 15 minutes, then reduce the heat to gas mark 4, 180°C (350°F) and bake for a further 30-40 minutes. The pie is best served hot.

A.W. : *A Book of Cookrye Very necessary for all such as delight therin*

36

EGGS IN MUSTARD SAUCE

Sodde Egges: Seeth your Egges almost harde, then peele them and cut them in quarters, then take a little butter in a frying panne and melt it a little broune, then put to it in to the panne, a little Vinegar, Mustarde, Pepper and Salte, and then put it into a platter upon your Egges.

For each egg take:

25 g (1 oz) butter
5 ml (1 tsp) made mustard
5 ml (1 tsp) vinegar
a pinch of salt
pepper to taste

Boil the eggs for 5 minutes. Meanwhile, lightly brown the butter in a small pan and allow it to cool a little before quickly stirring in the remaining ingredients. When the eggs are ready, peel and quarter them on a warm dish. Reheat the sauce, and pour it over the eggs immediately before serving.

J. Partridge: *The Widowes Treasure*

SPINACH FLAN

To make a tarte of Spinnage: Take three handfull of Spinnage, boil it in faire water, when it is boyled, put away the water from it and put the Spinnage in a stone morter, grind it smal with two dishes of butter melted, and foure rawe egges all to beaten, then straine it and season it with suger, sinamon and ginger, and lay it in your Coffin, when it is hardened in the oven, then bake it, and when it is enough, serve it upon a faire dish, and cast upon it Suger and Biskets.

Shortcrust pastry made with 100 g (4 oz) plain flour, 25 g (1 oz) lard and 25 g (1 oz) margarine
100 g (4 oz) fresh spinach or 275 g (10 oz) can spinach, drained
3 eggs
50 g (2 oz) butter, melted
5 ml (1 tsp) cinnamon
5 ml (1 tsp) ground ginger
sugar, to finish (optional)

Line a 15 cm (6 in) flan ring with the pastry, and bake blind for 10-15 minutes at gas mark 7, 220°C (425°F). Wash the fresh spinach and pack into a saucepan with only the water that clings to the leaves, slowly bring to the boil, stirring occasionally, and simmer for 10-15 minutes until tender. Drain the spinach, and allow to cool before blending with the remaining ingredients to produce a smooth dark green mixture. Spread this evenly in the prepared flan and bake for 30-40 minutes at gas mark 4, 180°C (350°F). Sugar may be sprinkled over the flan just before it is served.

Thomas Dawson:
The good huswifes Jewell, pt. 2

SALAD

Take your hearbes and pick them very fine into fair water and pick your flowers by themselves, and wash them al cleane, and swing them in a strainer, and when you put them into the dish, mingle them with Cowcumbers or Lemmans payred and sliced, and scrape Sugar, and put in Vinegar and Oyle and throw the flowers on the top of the sallet and of every sorte of the aforesaide thinges and garnish the dish about with the foresaid thinges and hard Egges boyled and laid about the dish and upon the sallet.

Lettuce (or mixed leaves of rocket, herbs, etc)
Flower heads (nasturtiums, violets, etc)
1 cucumber (or lemon if preferred)
60 ml (4 tbs) olive oil
45 ml (3 tbls) red wine vinegar
2.5 ml ('/2 tsp) salt
1.5 ml ('/4 tsp) brown sugar
8 hard-boiled eggs

Wash and dry the lettuce leaves and tear or slice into small pieces. Peel and slice the cucumber (or lemon) and quarter the hard-boiled eggs. Mix up the oil, vinegar, salt and sugar. Place the salad leaves in a dish, sprinkle over the oil dressing and decorate with the egg quarters and flowers.

Thomas Dawson:
The good huswifes Jewell, pt. 1

41

BOILED ONIONS

To boile Onions: Take a good many onions and cut them in four quarters, set them on the fire in as much water as you think will boyle them tender, and when they be clean skinned, put in a good many raisons, halfe a spooneful of grose pepper, a good peece of Suger, and a little Salt, and when the Onions be through boiled, beat the yolke of an Egge with Vergious, and put into your pot and so serve it upon soppes. If you will, poch Egges and lay upon them.

450 g (1 lb) onions, peeled and quartered
75 g (3 oz) raisins
5 ml (1 tsp) pepper
15 ml (1 tbls) sugar
2.5 ml (½ tsp) salt
275 ml (½ pt) water
1 egg yolk
15 ml (1 tbls) cider vinegar
225 g (8 oz) bread, cut into crustless cubes
poached eggs (optional)

Simmer the onions, raisins, pepper, sugar and salt in the water for 10-15 minutes, until the onions are tender. Beat the egg yolk and cider vinegar together, and stir into the onions to thicken the liquid. Serve on a bed of cubes of bread, and top with poached eggs if a more substantial dish is required.

Thomas Dawson:
The good huswifes Jewell, pt. 2

THICK PEA POTTAGE

To boyle yong Peason or Beanes:
First shale them and seethe them in
faire water, then take them out of the
water and put them into boyling
milk, then take the yolks of Egs with
crums of bread, and ginger, and
straine them thorow a strainer with
the said milk, then take chopped
percely, Saffron and Salt, and serve
it foorth for Pottage.

25 g (1 oz) fresh breadcrumbs
1 egg yolk
5 ml (1 tsp) chopped parsley
5 ml (1 tsp) salt
2.5 ml (1/2 tsp) ground ginger
a pinch of saffron
275 ml (1/2 pt) milk
350 g (12 oz) cooked peas, or
525 g (19 oz) can of peas

Beat together the breadcrumbs, egg yolk, parsley, salt, ginger and saffron. Bring the milk almost to the boil, pour in the peas and the breadcrumb mixture, then bring to the boil over a low heat, stirring continuously. This thick pottage can be used as a quickly made and very substantial warming soup, or it may be served as a vegetable, making an excellent accompaniment to fish dishes.

A.W. : *A Book of Cookrye Very*
necessary for all such as delight therin

APPLE MOUSSE

To make Apple Moyse: Take a dozen apples and ether rooste or boyle them and drawe them thorowe a streyner, and the yolkes of three or foure egges withal, and, as ye strayne them, temper them wyth three or foure sponefull of damaske water yf ye wyll, than take and season it wyth suger and halfe a dysche of swete butter, and boyle them upon a chaffyngdysche in a platter, and caste byskettes or synamon and gynger upon them and so serve them forth.

700 g (1 ½ lb) apples
45 ml (3 tbls) water
2 egg yolks
30 ml (2 tbls) rosewater
30 ml (2 tbls) sugar
25 g (1 oz) butter
ground ginger and cinnamon, to finish

Peel, core and slice the apples, and stew them with the water until soft in a heavy covered saucepan. Make the apples into a smooth purée by either rubbing through a sieve or using a blender. Return the purée to the saucepan, stir in the egg yolks beaten with the rosewater, then the sugar and the butter, and slowly heat to boiling point, stirring continuously. Pour the purée into a dish and allow to cool before serving. To finish, sprinkle with a little ground ginger and cinnamon.

A Proper Newe Book of Cokerye

PRUNE TART

To make a Tarte of Prunes: Take Prunes and wash them, then boil them with faire water, cut in halfe a peny loaf of white bread, and take them out and strain them with Claret wine, season it with sinamon, Ginger and Sugar, and a little Rosewater, make the paste as fine as you can, and dry it, and fill it, and let it drie in the oven, take it out and cast on it Biskets and Carawaies.

350 g (12 oz) prunes
100 g (4 oz) fresh white
   breadcrumbs
275 ml (¹/₂ pt) red wine
5 ml (1 tsp) cinnamon
5 ml (1 tsp) ground ginger
100 g (4 oz) sugar
15 ml (1 tbls) rosewater

For the pastry:

75 g (3 oz) butter
100 g (4 oz) plain flour
5 ml (1 tsp) caster sugar
1 egg, beaten

Soak the prunes overnight, then simmer in a little water for 10-15 minutes until tender. To make the pastry, rub the butter into the flour, mix in the sugar, and slowly stir in the eggs until it forms a soft dough which can be lightly kneaded with the hands. Roll out the pastry, and use it to line a 20 cm (8 in) diameter, 5 cm (2 in) deep flan ring. Line the pastry with greaseproof paper, fill with uncooked haricot beans or crusts, and bake blind at gas mark 7, 220°C (425°F) for 15 minutes. Remove the beans and greaseproof paper. To make the filling, drain and stone the prunes, then blend them with the remaining ingredients to form a smooth thick paste. Spoon the filling into the pastry case, and return to the oven to bake at gas mark 4, 180°C (350°F) for 1½ hours. Serve either hot or cold.

A.W. : *A Book of Cookrye Very necessary for all such as delight therin*

PRUNES IN SYRUP

To make Prunes in sirrope: Take Prunes, and put Claret wine to them, and Sugar, as much as you think will make them pleasant, let all these seeth together till yee thinke the liquor looke like a sirrope, and that your Prunes be well swollen: and so keepe them in a vessell as yee doe greene Ginger.

225 g (8 oz) prunes
425 ml (³/₄ pt) claret
100 g (4 oz) sugar

Soak the prunes overnight in the claret, then simmer the prunes, claret and sugar for 10-15 minutes until the prunes are fully swollen and tender. They may then be eaten directly, or sealed into sterilised jars for use at a future time.

J. Partridge: *The Treasurie of Commodious Conceites and Hidden Secrets*

This rich but simple dish provides a convenient example of the 'suckets' eaten with a fork during the banquet course.

Opposite: Orange and lemon slices also make excellent 'suckets'

SWEET CUBES OF JELLIED MILK

A white leach: Take a quart of newe milke, and three ounces weight of Isinglasse, half a pounde of beaten suger, and stirre them together, and let it boile half a quarter of an hower till it be thicke, stirring them al the while: then straine it with three sponfull of Rosewater, then put it into a platter and let it coole, and cut it in squares. Lay it faire in dishes, and lay golde upon it.

25 ml (5 tsps) gelatine
575 ml (1 pt) milk
100 g (4 oz) sugar
25 ml (5 tsps) rosewater

Sprinkle the gelatine on to 60 ml (4 tbls) of the milk in a cup. Leave for 5 minutes before standing the cup in hot water and stirring the gelatine until it is completely dissolved. Warm the remaining milk, stir in the gelatine and the sugar, and simmer, stirring continuously, for 5 minutes. Remove from the heat, stir in the rosewater, and pour into a shallow baking dish about 15 cm (6 in) square which has been freshly rinsed in cold water. Allow to set firmly in a cool place before cutting into squares with a sharp knife. The squares may then be either arranged in a regular pattern or stacked as a pyramid on a flat plate ready for the table.

Thomas Dawson:
The good huswifes Jewell, pt. 2

This unusual dish has a delicious, cool sweet flavour and a translucent ivory-white appearance similar to Turkish delight.

POSSET

To make a good Possett Curde: First take the Milke and seeth it on the fire, and before it seeth put in your Egges according to the quantitye of your Milke, but see that your Egges be tempered with some of your milke that standeth on the fire, and you must stirre it still untill it seeth, and beginning to rise, then take it from the fire, and have your drinke ready in a fair Bason on a chafing dishe of coles and put your Milke in to the bason as it standeth, and cover it, and let it stand a while, then take it up, and cast on ginger and synomon.

Beat the eggs into the milk, and heat gently, stirring continuously, until the mixture has thickened and is about to rise to the boil. Meanwhile, heat the ale almost to boiling point and pour into a large warmed bowl. Quickly pour the hot egg and milk mixture into the ale from a good height, cover the bowl and leave in a warm place for 5 minutes to allow the curd to set. Sprinkle a little cinnamon and ginger over the posset, which is now ready to be served.

J. Partridge: *The Widowes treasure*

3 eggs
575 ml (1 pt) milk
275 ml (¹/₂ pt) strong brown ale
cinnamon and ground ginger

Simple possets of this type became much richer and sweeter as they grew in popularity in the later 17th century.

PEARS IN SYRUP

*To conserve wardens all the yeere in
sirrop: Take your wardens and put
them into a great Earthen pot, and
cover them close, set them in an Oven
when you have set in your white
bread, & when you have drawne your
white bread, and your pot, & that
they be so colde as you may handle
them, then pill the thin skinne from
them over a pewter dish, that you
may save all the sirroppe that falleth
from them: put to them a quarte of
the same sirrope, and a pinte of
Rosewater, and boile them together
with a fewe Cloves and Sinnamon,
and when it is reasonable thick and
cold, put your wardens and Sirroppe
into a Galley pot and see alwaies that
the Syrrop bee above the Wardens, or
any other thing that you conserve.*

1.3 kg (3 lb) pears
850 ml (1 1/2 pt) water
225 g (8 oz) sugar
150 ml (1/4 pt) rosewater
5 ml (1 tsp) whole cloves
2 sticks cinnamon

Place the pears in a casserole and bake
at gas mark 4, 180°C (350°F) for 1-1 1/2
hours until soft to the touch. Cool,
then peel. Simmer any liquor which
runs from them with a syrup made
from the remaining ingredients, add the
pears, and simmer for a few minutes
before cooling.

Thomas Dawson:
The good huswifes Jewell, pt. 2

JUMBLES OR KNOTTED BISCUITS

To make Iombils a hundred: Take twenty Egges and put them into a pot both the yolkes & the white, beat them wel, then take a pound of beaten suger and put to them, and stirre them wel together, then put to it a quarter of a peck of flower, and make a hard paste thereof, and then with Anniseeds moulde it well, ane make it in little rowles beeing long, and tye them in knots, and wet the ends in Rosewater, then put them into a pan of seething water, but even in one waum, then take them out with a Skimmer and lay them in a cloth to drie, this being don lay them in a tart panne, the bottome beeing oyled, then put them into a temperat Oven for one howre, turning them often in the Oven.

2 eggs
100 g (4 oz) sugar
15 ml (1 tbls) aniseed or caraway
175 g (6 oz) plain flour

Beat the eggs in a large basin, then beat in the sugar, the aniseed or caraway, and finally the flour, thus forming a stiff dough. Knead the dough on a lightly floured board, and form into rolls approximately 1 cm ($^3/_8$ in) in diameter by 10 cm (4 in) in length. Tie each of these in a simple knot and plunge them, five or six at a time, into a pan of boiling water, where they will immediately sink to the bottom. After a short time dislodge the knots from the bottom of the pan with a spoon so that they float and swell for a minute or two. Then lift the knots out with a

perforated spoon, and allow them to drain on a clean tea-towel laid over a wire rack. Arrange the knots on lightly buttered baking sheets and bake for 15 minutes at gas mark 4, 180°C (350°F), then turn the knots over and return to the oven for 10–15 minutes until golden.

Thomas Dawson:
The good huswifes Jewell, pt. 2

TRIFLE

To make Trifle: Take a pinte of thicke creame, and season it with Sugar and Ginger, and Rosewater, so stirre it as you would them have it, and make it luke warme in a dish on a chafingdishe and coales, and after put it into a silver peece or a bowle, and so serve it to the boorde.

750 ml (1 ¼ pt) double cream
22.5 ml (1 ½ tbls) sugar
22.5 ml (1 ½ tbls) rosewater
3.5 ml (¾ tsp) ground ginger

Beat the cream until it forms soft peaks, add sugar and other ingredients and continue beating until thick. Serve with wafers or shortbread biscuits.

This can be gently heated as in the original recipe or served cold.

Thomas Dawson:
The good huswifes Jewell, pt. 1

SUGAR PLATES AND WINE GLASSES

To make a paste of Suger, whereof a man may make al manner of fruits, and other fine thinges with their forme, as Plates, Dishes, Cuppes, and such like thinges, wherewith you may furnish a Table: Take Gumme and dragant as much as you wil, and steep it in Rosewater till it be mollified, and for four ounces of suger take of it the bignes of a beane, the juyce of Lemons, a walnut shel ful, and a little of the white of an eg. But you must first take the gumme, and beat it so much with a pestell in a brasen morter, till it be come like water, then put in the juyce with the white of an egge, incorporating al these wel together, this don take four ounces of fine white suger well beaten to powder, and cast it into ye morter

by a little and little until they be turned into ye form of paste, then take it out of the said morter, and bray it upon the powder of suger, as it were meale or flower, untill it be like soft paste, to the end you may turn it, and fashion it which way you wil. When you have brought your paste to this fourme spread it abroad upon great or smal leaves as you shall thinke it good, and so shal you form or make what things you wil, as is aforesaid, with such fine knackes as may serve a Table taking heede there stand no hotte thing nigh it. At the end of the Banket they may eat all, and break the Platters, Dishes, Glasses, Cuppes, and all other things, for this paste is very delicate and saverous.

2.5 ml ($^1/_2$ tsp) gelatine
5 ml (1 tsp) lemon juice
10 ml (2 tsps) rosewater
$^1/_2$ egg white, lightly beaten
350–450 g (12–16 oz) icing sugar

Stir the gelatine into the lemon juice and rosewater in a basin and place over a bowl of hot water until melted. Stir in the lightly beaten egg white, and work in the icing sugar, little by little, until a dough is formed. It can then be turned out on a board dusted with icing sugar, and kneaded until completely smooth. Having dusted the board with a little cornflour, the mixture is then rolled out thinly and pressed into saucers, plates, or the bowls of wine glasses to mould it into the required shapes. The surplus trimmed from the rims may then be modelled in the form of baluster stems and bases, either for the glasses or to convert the saucers into standing tazzas for the better display of sweetmeats. A little royal icing can be used to join the various sections together after they have been allowed to dry and harden for a few hours. Glasses and dishes made in this porcelain-like translucent material can provide an interesting range of vessels for the presentation of any cold dry sweetmeats on the banqueting table. Sugar wine glasses filled with crystallised flowers make a particularly elegant display, the contrast of textures and colours bringing a rare beauty to the table.

Thomas Dawson:
The good huswifes Jewell, pt. 2

59

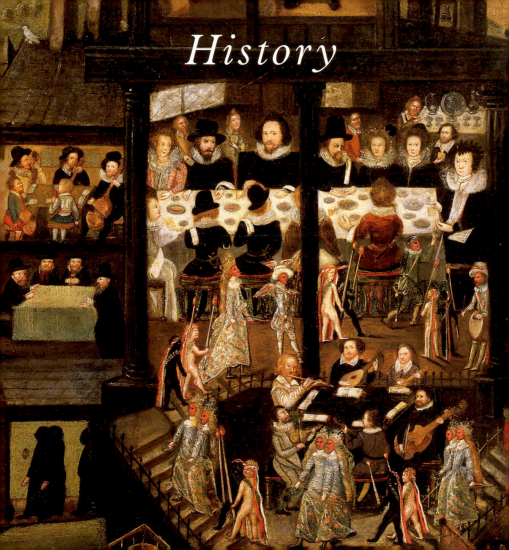

CULINARY ORGANISATION IN THE GREAT HOUSEHOLDS

As in most aspects of fashionable Tudor life, the sovereign and the courtiers set the required standards of taste in all aspects of cookery and eating habits. At the court itself, based in one of the massive palaces at Whitehall, Richmond, Hampton Court, Nonsuch or Greenwich, vast quantities of high-quality food had to be prepared for perhaps 1,500 or more diners every day. It was therefore essential that each establishment was provided with vast series of domestic buildings, including cellars for the storage of beer and wine, pantries and larders for the storage of food, spacious bake-houses, and kitchens lined with wide-arched fireplaces where roasting and boiling could be undertaken.

Similar facilities, albeit on a somewhat smaller scale, were also necessary in the magnificent houses then being erected by the great land-owning families. Mansions such as Burghley, Hardwick,

Opposite: Detail of the *Wedding Feast of Sir Henry Unton*, unknown artist, *c.*1596. Note the symmetrical arrangement of the dishes, the square trenchers and the diners' habit of folding their napkins over their forearms

> '**Cookery is become an art, a noble science; cooks are gentlemen.**'
>
> Robert Burton 1577-1640,
> *Anatomy of Melancholy*

Longleat, Wollaton and Cowdray all incorporated excellent catering facilities capable of dealing with both their own everyday requirements, and also the enormous demands occasioned by the visits of the court during one of its annual progressions through the country. In these houses, the whole of the domestic management was placed in the hands of a senior member of the resident staff, usually the steward. The actual control of the kitchens, provisions, and kitchen staff was then delegated to a clerk in the kitchen. The full extent of this officer's responsibilities, and also the complex workings of a great Tudor establishment are well illustrated in the *Booke of the Household of Queene Elizabeth* of 1600.

Working under the direction of the Lord Chamberlain, the Clerk to the Kitchen controlled a total staff of 160, his eleven chief officers, either serjeants, chief clerks or master cooks, each contributing the services of their specialist departments. The Serjeant of the Accatry, for example, was responsible for gathering beef and mutton from the queen's pastures, together with veal, pork, lard, sea fish, freshwater fish and salt. These were all passed to the Serjeant of the Larder, whose Yeoman of the Boyling House boiled them as required. It is probable that the actual boilers were large permanent vessels of copper or brass encased within masonry structures and heated by means of

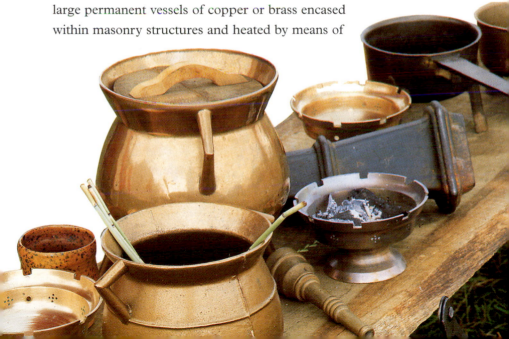

Culinary organisation in the great households

The 16th-century *Ordinance of the Bakers of York* depicting different stages in the making of bread

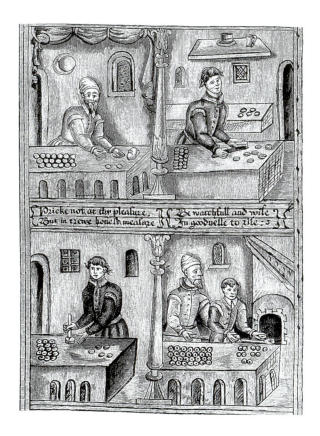

their own fireplaces and flues. Smaller quantities of meat would be boiled in metal cauldrons hung from a bar fixed across the chimney in a normal fireplace. Poultry, game birds and lambs were the responsibility of the Serjeant of the Poultry, whose Yeoman of the Scalding House scalded, plucked and drew them ready for the cooks. The Serjeant of the Bakehouse, meanwhile, had a Yeoman Garnetor to maintain supplies of corn and flour, Yeoman Pervayers who carried supplies into the bakehouses, and further yeomen and grooms who baked bread for both the queen's table and the entire household.

The workings of bakehouses at this period are clearly seen in the *Ordinance of the Bakers of York* (see opposite). After measuring and milling the grain, the flour was boulted or sieved to remove the bran. This was done by shaking a quantity of flour through a piece of coarse canvas or linen – probably from Doulas in Brittany – the 'dowlas' which Falstaff gave away to bakers' wives to make boulters of in Shakespeare's *Henry IV, Part I*. The fine flour was then swept up with a small broom and a goosewing, and kneaded with salt, yeast and water in a long wooden dough-trough. After being worked into loaves and carefully weighed, the dough was next pricked or marked, allowed to rise, and slipped into the oven by means of a long oven-slice or peel. The oven itself was of the bee-hive variety, consisting of a large domed masonry structure, entered by way of a small rectangular door. A fire of fast-burning kindling was first lit inside the oven so that its floor, walls and roof were brought up to a high temperature. The fire was then raked out, the bread swiftly inserted, and the oven door sealed in place with mud. After a short while, the oven door was broken open, and the bread, baked by the heat retained by the masonry, withdrawn and allowed to cool. Similar ovens were

A London bakehouse, where the baker uses a long wooden peel to place the bread in a bee-hive oven

used by the Serjeant of the Pastry, who prepared all the baked meats, pastries and pies, ensuring that they were 'well seasoned with that proportion of spice which is allowed them, and well-filled, and made according to the rate which is appointed unto them ... and see that no waste be made of sauces'. In the Spicery, meanwhile, the Chief Clarke controlled the finer aspects of bakery, with yeomen to beat the spice into powder, using pestle and mortar, yeomen to make wafers for festivals with beautifully decorated iron wafer-tongs, and further yeomen to run the Confectionary which supplied pears, wardens, figs, raisins and other fruit.

The provision of all the equipment used throughout the royal kitchens was the responsibility of the Serjeant of the Scullery. As well as issuing 'chistes, guarde or irons, tubbes, trayes, baskets, flaskets [long shallow baskets], scoopes, broaches [spits], peeles and such like', he had full charge of all the silver and pewter dishes and candlesticks used on the royal tables.

By combining these facilities with those of their own kitchens, the master cooks for the queen and her household were admirably equipped to prepare the elaborate dishes required by the court. In addition to the usual range of utensils, such as knives, spoons,

whisks made of bundles of blanched twigs, and a variety of bowls and colanders, the master cook's most useful resource was probably the stove. This was a long masonry bench or worktop, into which was set a number of round firebaskets lined with sheet iron. Fuelled with charcoal, the stove could be used just like one of today's gas or electric stoves, allowing small quantities of food to be heated either fiercely or gently, perhaps in a saucepan or a frying pan, while being stirred or beaten by the cook. Close control of this type was essential when making sauces, egg dishes or many of the sugar-based preserves and confections.

The preparation of fine food was by no means restricted only to the professional cooks employed in the great households as Lucy Aikin noted (see p71). In this way, the knowledge of the court cooks, exclusively male throughout the Middle Ages, was passed into the hands of the English gentlewomen, who were to develop it to an outstanding degree over the coming centuries.

When a meal was to be served in the royal household, the Serjeant of the Pantry was responsible for the Yeomen for the

Opposite: View of the kitchen at Cotehele, Cornwall

Mouthe, the grooms and pages who took the bread, salt, trenchers and cutlery to her majesty's table before carrying up the main courses. The Serjeant of the Seller, meanwhile, took charge of all liquid refreshment. His Yeoman of the Pitcher-house provided the silver drinking vessels, jacks and cups, in which wines from the cellar and other drinks from the buttery were served by further Yeomen for the Mouthe.

The process of laying the royal table was then carried out with great pomp and ceremony, even though the queen was never present. First two gentlemen entered the room, one bearing a rod, and the other a tablecloth, which, after they had both kneeled three times, with the utmost veneration, was spread upon the table. After kneeling again, they then retired to be followed by two others, one with the rod again, the other with a salt-cellar, a plate and bread; when they had kneeled, as the others had done, and placed what was brought upon the table, they too retired, with the same ceremonies performed by the first gentlemen. At last came an unmarried lady, dressed in white silk, along with a married one bearing a tasting knife; the former prostrated herself three times, and in the most graceful manner approached the table where she

'Many of the elder sort of courtier ladies were also [in addition to languages, music and needlework] skilful in surgery and the distilation of waters ... each of them cunning in something whereby they keep themselves occupied in the court, there is a manner none of them but when they be at home can help to supply the ordinary want of the kitchen with a number of delicate dishes of their own devising, wherein the portingal [Portuguese] is their chief counsellor; as some of them are most commonly with the clerk of the kitchen.'

Lucy Aikin, *Memoirs of the Court of Queen Elizabeth*, 1819

carefully rubbed the plates with bread and salt. When they had waited there a little time, the yeomen of the guard entered bareheaded, clothed in scarlet with a golden rose upon their backs, bringing in at each turn a course of twenty-four dishes, served in silver plate, most of it gilt. These dishes were received by a gentleman in the same order, who brought them in and placed them upon the table, while the lady taster gave to each of the guard a mouthful to eat, for fear of any poison. During the time that this guard (which consisted of the tallest and stoutest men that could be found in all England) were bringing dinner, twelve trumpets and two kettle-drums made the hall ring for half an hour altogether. At the end of all this ceremonial, a number of unmarried ladies appeared, who with particular solemnity lifted the meat off the table and conveyed it to the queen's inner and more private chamber, where, after she had chosen for herself, the remainder went to the ladies of the court. On important state occasions, however, the monarch dined in formal state with her courtiers either in the Presence Chamber or some similarly impressive apartment.

Opposite: A 16th-century state banquet serving peacock

THE MEALS

In most noble establishments the full medieval ceremonials, menus, courses, and methods of service continued virtually unchanged throughout the 16th century, except for one notable detail. Instead of dining at the head of the entire household in the great hall, the lord, his family, and the officers who served him at table now withdrew into their more private great chambers or 'dining chambers'. They still dined in the hall on all major state occasions or feasts, however, including royal visits, Christmastime, weddings or funerals. There was a tendency though to decrease and regulate

On the Twelfth Day of Christmas it was a tradition to slice a special cake which had been baked with a bean inside and distribute portions among the children and servants of the household. Whoever found the bean could rule for the rest of the day and night as King of the Bean.

Opposite: Elizabeth I takes breakfast before the hunt, 1575

'Good bread and good drink,
A good fire in the hall,
Brawn, pudding and souse,
And good mustard withal.
Beef, mutton and pork,
And good pies of the best,
Pig, veal, goose and capon,
And turkey well drest,
Cheese, apples and nuts,
And good carols to hear,
As then in the country
Is counted good cheer.'

Thomas Tusser, *500 Points of Husbandry*, 1573

the number of meals served throughout the day: 'Whereas of old we had breakfasts in the forenoon, beverages or nunchions after dinner, and thereto rear-suppers, generally when it was time to go to rest, now these odd repasts, thanked be to God, are very well left, and each one in manner contenteth himself with dinner and supper only.' For the gentry, dinner was served at eleven in the morning and supper between five and six in the evening, but on special occasions these meals could be extended by 'banquets'.

After the main meal had been cleared from the Presence Chamber at York Place (now St James's Palace) a group of masquers disguised as shepherds entered with a flourish of hautboys. As Cardinal Wolsey recognised Henry VIII among the unexpected party, he called to Sir Thomas Lovell, 'Is the banquet ready i'th Privy Chamber?' Here he was referring to the banquet in its original 16th-century form, when it was served as an elaborate dessert course of sweetmeats, fruits and wine, either as a meal in itself or as a continuation of dinner or supper, set out in a separate apartment. While Wolsey retired to his Privy Chamber, other noble hosts might go up to the ornate banqueting houses which rose above the leads of their house roofs, as at Longleat, Hardwick,

Lavender, and other sweet-smelling herbs, were used to decorate bowers used for elaborate banquets

or Lacock Abbey, or perhaps proceed to delightful banqueting houses or lodges erected in some secluded corner of their park. These detached structures might be built in permanent masonry, but frequently they were 'made with fir poles and decked with birch branches and all manner of flowers both of the field and of the garden, as roses, julyflowers, lavender, marygolds, and all manner of strewing herbs and rushes' – such as Elizabeth caused to be erected in Greenwich Park for the reception of the French Embassy in 1560.

The banquet provided the greatest opportunity for the display of wealth, colour, ingenuity and culinary splendour. At Kenilworth, Robert Dudley's entertainment for the queen featured 'a most delicious and an ambrosial banquet; whereof whether I might muse at the daintiness, shapes, and the cost, or else, at the variety and number of the dishes (that were three hundred)'. *The Good Huswifes Closet* gives detailed instructions of how to make all kinds of banqueting stuff, including three-dimensional birds, beasts and fruits in cast sugar, or pies, birds and baskets in marzipan. Even the wine glasses, dishes, playing cards and trenchers were made of a crisp modelled sugar called sugar-plate. This could be elaborately decorated with colourful brush and penwork enriched with bright gilding. Although all the sugar-plate trenchers disappeared centuries ago, we can gain an exact impression of their appearance from their surviving alternatives made of sycamore. Measuring some five inches in diameter, one of their sides was left plain, to provide a surface from which to eat fruits, sweetmeats or cheese, while the other bore floral and strapwork motifs and a suitable inscription. George Puttenham's *Art of English Poesie* of 1589 describes the 'epigrams that were sent usually for New Yeares gifts or to be printed or put upon their banketting dishes of sugar plate or of March paines … they were called "Apophereta" and never contained above one verse or two at the most, but the shorter the better. We call them poesies, and do paint them now a dayes upon the backe sides of our fruit trenchers of wood.'

In addition to taking part in outdoor banquets, the Tudor monarchs also enjoyed the elaborate breakfasts which preceded the hunt. The English were known throughout Europe for their love of field sports, and most of the royal palaces and great houses had a deer park dotted with clumps of trees and enclosed by a high wooden fence. While visiting Viscount Montagu, Elizabeth rode

A contemporary description of the many gifts presented to Queen Elizabeth I over the New Year celebrations of 1561–2 included a chessboard from George Webster, her Master Cook. Not only could she play a game with it – she could also eat it! Webster had coloured and moulded almond paste to form this unusual 'marchpane', a marzipan-like confection that was a popular centrepiece at many Tudor banquets.

Opposite: A 'marchpane' in the form of a Tudor rose

out into the park where a delicate bower had been prepared for her reception. Here a nymph with a sweet song presented her with a crossbow which she used expertly to despatch three or four deer driven across her view. On these hunting days the preparations for the entertainment of the queen started when the butler set off into the park with a train of waggons, carts and pack-mules carrying all the necessary food and drink to the place of assembly. This location was carefully chosen to ensure adequate shade beneath stately trees, with an array of wild flowers, a nearby spring of clear water, and sweet singing birds to make melody. The butler's first task was to place bottles and barrels of beer and wine into the spring to cool:

> *That doone: he spreades his cloth, upon the grassye banke,*
> *And sets to shewe his deintie drinkes, to winne his Princes thanke.*
> *Then commes the captain Cooke, with many a warlike wight,*
> *Which armor bring and weapons both, with hunger for to fight …*

For whiles colde loynes of Veale, cold Capon, Beefe and Goose,
With Pygeon pyes, and Mutton colde, are set on hunger
   loose …
First Neates tongs poudred well, and Gambones of the Hogge,
Then Saulsages and savery knacke, to set mens myndes
   on gogge …
Then King or comely Queene, then Lord and Lady looke,
To see which side will bear the bell, the Butler or the Cooke.
At last the Cooke takes flight, the Butlers still abyde,
And sound their Drummes and make retreat, with bottles by
   their syde.

The assembled hunters then presented the queen with accounts of the various deer they had located, together with samples of droppings, so that she might select the quarry for the day, and so the hunt commenced.

This stag was scratched on the side of the serving hatch in the kitchens of Hampton Court and probably represents royal venison

TABLEWARE

Wherever the meal was to be served, the tableware used in royal and noble households was always of the finest quality. Following the medieval tradition, the great continued to eat from vessels made in gold, silver-gilt or silver. All their magnificent chargers, standing cups and ewers worked in these precious metals were intended for show as much as for use. Henry VIII displayed a cupboard of twelve shelves all filled with plate of gold at his feasts, while George Cavendish, in his *Life of Cardinal Wolsey*, described the proud prelate's 'Cup Board made for the Chamber, in length of the breadth of the nether end of the same Chamber, six desks [i.e. shelves] high, full of gold plate, very sumptuous, and of the newest fashions, and upon the nethermost desk garnished all with gold, most curiously wrought … This Cup Board was barred in round about that no man might come nigh it.' The number of shelves was quite significant, dukes being permitted four or five, lesser noblemen three, knights banneret two, and ordinary gentlemen one.

Opposite: A plate and spoons from the pewter collection at Arlington Court, Devon

On the table, pride of place was still occupied by the great salt, which formed the principal decoration, and was the first vessel to be set in place once the cloth had been laid. In shape it could vary considerably, but it was quite tall, raised on ornate feet, and had its gilt bowl surmounted by a high canopy or cover. Around the table much smaller trencher salts might also be provided for less important diners and members of the household.

The 16th century saw the decline of the medieval practice of serving food on square-cut trenchers made of wholemeal bread. These were largely replaced by the sops of bread which were now arranged in the dish beneath boiled or stewed meats before they were brought to table. The trencher continued in a rather different form, however, for it changed into a thin square wooden board,

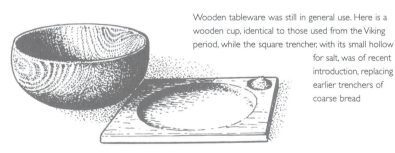

Wooden tableware was still in general use. Here is a wooden cup, identical to those used from the Viking period, while the square trencher, with its small hollow for salt, was of recent introduction, replacing earlier trenchers of coarse bread

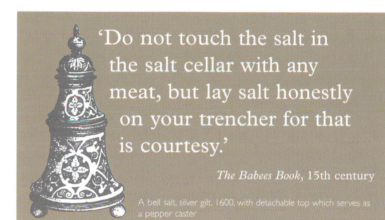

'Do not touch the salt in the salt cellar with any meat, but lay salt honestly on your trencher for that is courtesy.'

The Babees Book, 15th century

A bell salt, silver gilt, 1600, with detachable top which serves as a pepper caster

one side of which was turned down to form two shallow recesses. The large central hollow, measuring five or six inches in diameter, contained the meat and gravy, while the smaller one, situated at one corner, held the diner's own supply of salt. Further changes in tableware occurred when Jasper Andries and Jacob Jansen came from Antwerp in 1567 to establish tin-glazed earthenware potteries in Norwich and London. Unlike the native English wares, their products had a smooth glossy white surface capable of being painted with metallic oxides to give colourful permanent decoration in the most fashionable Renaissance style.

The materials and design of drinking vessels also made great leaps forward during this period. While silver and gold remained popular with the wealthy, and horn beakers and black leather jacks continued to be used by the poor, important changes were imminent. Already by 1500, the traditional ashwood drinking cups, shallow turned bowls measuring some 15 cm (6 in) in diameter, on which Henry VIII expended £20 a year, were starting to be superseded by earthenware cups. In the south-east, they were made in vast quantities in the Surrey kilns, their 'Tudor Green' forms having a brilliant copper-green glaze over a finely-thrown creamy-buff fabric. In the northern counties, the cups were made of a hard-fired dark red fabric, glazed to a glossy dark brown or black, and decorated with flowers, stags' heads and stamped pads of white clay. This type of pottery is now known as Cistercian Ware since it was first discovered during the excavation of Cistercian monasteries in Yorkshire about a century ago.

Glass too was becoming increasingly widespread. In 1575 the Venetian Jacomo Verzelini came from the Netherlands to establish

'It is a world to see in these our days how that the gentility do now generally choose rather the Venice glasses, both for our wine and beer. The poorest will also have glass if they may, but, sith the Venetian is somewhat too dear for them, they content themselves with such as are made at home of fern and burned stone.'

William Harrison,
Description of England, 1577

A glass tankard with silver-gilt mounts, made in the Venetian style in London, c. 1548

a glasshouse in London, where he began to produce bowls and glasses of the highest quality, their surfaces perhaps being elaborately engraved with the customer's coats of arms and initials. In the provinces, meanwhile, in Surrey and Sussex, the Bristol Channel area, Staffordshire, Lancashire, Cheshire and North Yorkshire, further glasshouses were soon employing local materials to make a wide range of goblets, bottles, distillation equipment and beer glasses. The last according to Sir Hugh Platt's *Jewell House of Art and Nature* were 'of six or eight inches in height and being of one equal bigness from the bottom to the top'.

An engraved wine glass made in the London glasshouse of Verzelini (1522-1616)

With regard to cutlery, the only significant development was the slow introduction of the fork. Henry VIII had owned 'suckett' forks, with a spoon at one end and a two-pronged fork at the other end of a single shaft, while Elizabeth began to receive New Year gifts of gold, silver and rock-crystal-handled forks from 1582. These were most probably used to eat the sticky sweetmeats served at banquets, for many years were to pass before the fork came into general use in this country.

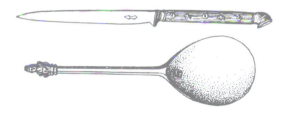

This silver maiden-head spoon of c.1540 and steel knife of the late 16th century both come from London

BIBLIOGRAPHY

Aiken, Lucy, *Memoirs of the Court of Queen Elizabeth* (London, 1819).

Anon, *The Boke of Cokery*, printed by Richard Pynson without Temple Bar (London, 1500) [The only known copy of this work is in the collection of the Marquis of Bath, Longleat House].

Anon, *The Book of Kervinge*, printed by Wynkyn de Worde (London, 1508) [Cambridge University Library Sel. 5.19.19].

Anon, *A Proper Newe Book of Cokerye*, printed by John Kynge & Thomas Marche (London, probably before 1572) [Corpus Christi College, Cambridge, Archbishop Parker Collection].

Anon, *The Good Hous-wives Treasurie*, printed by Edward Allde (London, 1588) [British Library 1038.d.43].

A.W., *A Book of Cookrye Very necessary for all such as delight therein*, printed by Edward Allde (London 1591) [Bodleian Library, Oxford, Douce W.23].

Boorde, Andrew, *A Compendyous Regyment or Dyetary of Helth*, printed by Robert Wyler (London, 1542).

Dawson, Thomas, *The good huswifes Jewell, part 1*, printed for Edward White (London, 1596); *part 2*, printed for Edward White by Edward Allde (London, 1597) [Bodleian Library, Oxford, Douce D.49 (1 & 2)].

Hope, W. H. St. John, *Cowdray and Easebourne Priory* (London 1919).

Partridge, J., *The Treasurie of Commodious Conceites and Hidden Secrets* (London, 1573, 1600).

Partridge, J., *The Widowes treasure . . .*, printed for Edward White by Robert Walde-grave (London, 1585) [Leeds University, Preston Collection P/K1 1585].

de Rosselli, Giovanni, *Epulario or the Italian Banquet wherein in shewn the maner how to dress ... all kinds of Flesh, Foules or Fishes,* translated from the original Italian and printed for William Barley by Abel Jeffes (London, 1598) [British Library 7955.b.8].

Society of Antiquaries, *A Collection of Ordinances and Regulations for the Government of the Royal Household* (London, 1790).

Turberville, George, *The Noble Arte of Venerie of Hunting* (London, 1575).

Wilson, C. Anne, *Food and Drink in Britain,* Constable (London, 1973).

ACKNOWLEDGEMENTS

The publishers would like to thank Historic Haut Cuisine for cooking and presenting a number of recipes featured in this book, and James O Davies and Peter Williams for photographing them. They are also grateful for the assistance given by Derry Brabbs in supplying photographs from his collection.

The publishers would like to thank the following people and organisations listed below for permission to reproduce the photographs in this book. Every care has been taken to trace copyright holders, but any omissions will, if notified, be corrected in any future edition.

All photographs are © English Heritage. NMR with the exception of the following:
Front cover: Longleat House, Wiltshire, UK/Bridgeman Art Library; pp12 & 13 Crown Copyright NFC; p17 Mary Evans Picture Library; p20 Derry Brabbs; p40 Derry Brabbs; p43 Derry Brabbs; p60 By courtesy of the National Portrait Gallery, London; p63 Derry Brabbs; p64 Private collection/Bridgeman Art Library; p68 National Trust Photographic Library/Andreas von Einsiedel; p84 National Trust Photographic Library/Nadia MacKenzie; p89 The British Museum, COMPASS; p90 V&A Images

Line illustrations by Peter Brears

RECIPE INDEX

In this Bermondsey cookshop c.1569, joints of meat can be seen roasting on spits in front of a roaring fire. In front, part of the wedding procession can be seen carrying great pasties, in long cloths around their necks

Other titles in this series:
Roman Cookery
Medieval Cookery
Stuart Cookery
Georgian Cookery
Victorian Cookery
Ration Book Cookery